THE BOOK OF THE

INTRODUCTION

Since the earlier days of my career, I have always dedicated myself to the study and application of technical subjects. With the creation of my startup MeetYourHero, I had the opportunity to learn more about what influencers and content creators do. Through an in-dept analysis of this field, which was a completely new experience for me, I quickly realized that, when lawfully and correctly practice, this career path can prove to be not only useful, but even necessary in present times. It is the new engine of the world, and also the noblest of Arts, since it is the fastest and most universal means of guaranteeing, everywhere, what is needed for the development of modern society. The well-being and modernity of a state mostly depends on the speed at which information is distributed among young people. Thus, the use of social media brings every globally available information available globally to the new generations, spreading innovative ideas in almost no time.

In this work, we're going to talk about the positive effects of influencer marketing and content creation. The content creator makes sure that information, news and ideas quickly reach every corner of the planet. By doing so, he manages to inspire anyone who has an Internet connection. More than anyone else, he's multifaceted, as he's the one who needs to be understood by different types of users the most. The perfect content creator must therefore have the ability to establish an empathetic connection with anyone on the other side of the screen, anywhere. Very soon I realized that the world of influencers is also crowded with ignorant and shallow people who act without scruples, in defiance of the laws of their country and making fun of their followers' trust. What is, to date, the noblest of Arts is sometimes used for vile purposes. This is why I wanted to write this book: to describe this activity according to its most beneficial role for society. Furthermore, this modern and yet traditional activity is not currently considered as a real job. In fact, it is mostly young people from Generation Z who consider it the basis of society and a useful and necessary tool for spreading universal knowledge. I hope this essay will help anyone who wants to understand – and maybe improve - such an essential contribution to modern society.

My main inspiration was merchant Benedetto Cotrugli's 13th-century text, an important work that influenced my business and to whose wisdom I am deeply grateful. I will use the same structure as that text in order to compare the merchant described by Cotrugli to the modern figure of the influencer.

Note: I will address my readers using the masculine form, as it is the standard in my native language, Italian, and I mean no disrespect to any gender identity.

Alessio Gaspari, founder of MeetYourHero
Vicenza (Italy) – November 19th, 2022

THE ART OF CHARISMATIC INFLUENCE

Influencer marketing is an art, that is, a discipline practiced by highly charismatic people who aim to spread economic and social ideas and behaviors to of their followers. Many usually start out in this field of work for fun, but always hoping to make money. Since earning is the ultimate goal of every influencer, I would like to analyze the activities that define this discipline.

The influencer is a modern entrepreneur, and as such follows many old and unwritten rules. There are some ethical constraints that may prevent some communities from working as influencers. There are those who can't do so without harming their followers, for instance by flaunting their (often exaggerated) wealth or by promoting unhealthy lifestyle. There are also people belonging to sacred order that consider it a vile, despicable act to profit off gullible followers by influencing their behavior with sketchy promises.

There's nothing else that could prevent anyone from becoming an influencer and – why not? – a good one. Influencers serve society by improving its living conditions. So, while this job started as a way to show off in front of a huge audience, over time it changed into an essential tool for spreading ideas, news, and culture.

Last but not least, influencers are starting to practice this new art hoping to earn money from it, which is exactly what happened with merchants in the past. In fact, the activity of purchasing and reselling goods by moving them from one place to another was born to satisfy human needs. Over the centuries, it proved to be very useful for merchants who managed to make good profits out of it. Similarly, influencers are like entrepreneurs in the sense that, by creating their own fanbase, they affect their followers' behavior and also earn money thanks to sponsorships and affiliations.

HOW TO BE A GOOD INFLUENCER

1 LET PEOPLE FIND YOU

Seneca said: "It is not the place that makes the man". Maybe he was right, but being found on social networks can make the difference between success and oblivion. While it may seem a trivial choice to make, the right social networks and the topics chosen for one's channel are very important things to worry about when starting out in this field. The same goes for the setting of the content creator's live streams: if possible, try to offer new settings to your followers in order to keep them motivated to follow you constantly. A great place to hang out and stream is the Houses of the Creators. If you regularly frequent these places, you will gradually become an expert and consequently richer. These Houses will also give you the opportunity to meet with other Creators and maybe collaborate with them. Furthermore, many of them have rooms available for guests who can stay for several days by accessing services such as the canteen, gym, showers and streaming stations. It's easy for many influencers to use their room as a recording studio, but remember not to isolate yourself. Don't close yourself off from the world, otherwise you risk isolating yourself, and you will only discover new trends once they've already started. When starting this activity it is also essential to evaluate and experiment the fields you are most suited to. In fact, while some are more suitable for the online gaming sector, others may be more drawn to fitness, cooking, and so on.

The same goes for the language used: some are very lucky to use local slang like a dialect, while others know and use English, the most commonly used lingua franca in the online environment. Still, others do not use any language and manage to appear more "universal". Furthermore, you need to look out for the future, for new niches of content to show to your followers in order to continuously improve engagement and the fanbase' appreciation. The same goes for new platforms on the market that could soon take away many followers from you, as trends in this area change every few months. Finally, you should keep in mind that a skilled influencer must also know how to change his business at the right moment, that is, when the profit decreases because there are too many competitors. Therefore, you should know how to come out of it in the best possible way.

2 BE CONFIDENT IN YOUR ABILITIES

Self-confidence means thinking you can handle difficult
situations. Having a high self-esteem instead means
positively evaluating one's personality. This involves
having a good opinion of oneself and acting in a stable
way in the face of unexpected events, difficulties and
hateful opinions. Self-confidence means being confident
and able to react, and is one of the main qualities of a
good influencer.
Trust yourself and don't let the haters bring you down, as
their comments are inevitable. However, don't be too
harsh; try and be polite with everyone, both followers and
haters, in a calm and respectful manner. Caution and
calmness are two virtues every good influencer should
have. In fact, while it is true that boldness brings about
many views, in the long run it keeps away those followers
who soon get tired of shallow and useless controversies
and go looking elsewhere for quality content. Caution is
an essential feature of honesty and includes knowing right
from wrong. It also consists in remembering the past,
valuing the present and providing for the future. In fact,
the mistakes influencers make often harm them more than
their followers.
Therefore, whoever practices this profession must have
his head on his shoulders and be able to do everything;
he must understand market trends and be cautious in
everything he does. Furthermore, he must be able to
make important decisions quickly. Above all, the
influencer must be smart and careful not to offend his

colleagues. He should also understand and take part in every new trend. The online entertainment market is super competitive and filled with pitfalls and fraudsters. In other words, the influencer must act rationally and in a professional way and accompanied by great seriousness and professionalism. Luck is just as helpful, especially in the case of people who act in a shrewd and responsible way.

The "balanced" influencer will therefore have to think on his own, first of all by keeping in mind what Lactantius said: "Everyone must trust in himself and that, for the research and evaluation of the truth, he has faith in his own judgment and understanding, rather than believing in the errors of others and being deceived, as if he were without reason. God has given all men the power of understanding, according to their ability, that they might investigate things unknown and bring those to scrutiny". It follows that, everyone is naturally intelligent, those who do not make good use of their judgment and approve the opinions of others without analyzing them, are led by others like sheep are led by a shepherd. In simpler words, "business doesn't want advice". I believe this saying to be true and important in modern entrepreneurship. While in politics good advisers are essential, in business they're counterproductive. In fact, it is not possible to analyze every decision: first of all because, if you have to ask for advice, the most suitable person will another influencer, to whom you will have to explain your idea at least in part. If you tell it in its entirety, it might be stolen from you; if you tell him only part of it, he won't have all the elements necessary to give you good advice. If, on the other hand, you want to ask someone who is not an influencer and therefore does not understand the principles of this job, you will have to explain everything and risk getting a not-so-great advice that may end up ruining your project.

A successful entrepreneur/influencer must have a lot of practice in examining, planning and predicting the future outcomes of each project he starts. This can only be achieved by gaining some experience in the field and studying the winning patterns of other influencers, even if they operate in different niches. Just like generals study the battlefield to come up with the best possible strategy, you must study the market to identify those potential business niches that haven't been exploited by competitors yet.

It is also very helpful to be balanced. Some are born that way, while others should strive as much as possible to act and offer content that is respectful pf everyone.

3 GET THROUGH HARD TIMES

Concentration and spirit of initiative, which are the cornerstones of the entrepreneurship, are not enough if the physical health of the entrepreneur/influencer is not adequately taken care of. If it seems strange to you that these issues are dealt with in a business book, you will change your mind when you discover how stressful the problems that the influencer has to face on a daily basis can be for the human body.

In fact, in order to make a good profit (which is the goal of every entrepreneur), it is necessary to take care of anything that somehow affects the final result. It is sometimes necessary to do work marathons, day and night, to be able to develop a good product that lives up to one's expectations. It may happen that, in order not to keep the flow of creativity going, essential activities such as eating, drinking and sleeping are postponed.

Two scenarios can arise from this: either the influencer fails to achieve his goal, or he risks burnout if he can't keep up anymore even if earns enough money. Since both cases can seriously damage one's finances and business continuity, they should be carefully avoided.

The best way to balance the working sphere with physical well-being is identifying an outdoor activity that can be carried out during both summer and winter and which allows the body and mind to recharge. I know many people who benefit a lot from taking a walk with their dog or cycling through the park to de-stress and clear their mind. Contact with nature is very effective in reducing stress levels; it also helps manage your psychological and physical well-being and balance your work and health. Find your best daily routine, even if it only lasts 20-30 minutes: even that short period of time can give you the opportunity to rebalance your strength and the ability to face your job in a more profitable way.

Set yourself ambitious goals, but remember to respect your body by taking a break from technology and the web at least once a day. I must also say that indoors physical activity is not have as beneficial as what is done outdoors. If you can, find your own little spot in a park, a meadow or in a forest nearby: I can assure you that you'll benefit a lot from this natural anti-stress practice.

4 FOCUS ON CONTENT

Don't try and do the impossible, let other influencers find their niche too. The online entertainment market is a multibillion-dollar business, and you can't expect to be able to satisfy everyone's needs. You should therefore learn to operate in such an overcrowded and competitive market. Seneca said, "It is proper to a spoiled stomach to taste many things", so concentrate on one or two business niches. Do not pursue, as many do, a thousand different areas just because they trend and seem more promising than those you're currently working on. Keep in mind that your fans follow you for the content, and you don't know if they'll keep following you once you explore different niches. Stay true to your field of expertise and interests. As a couple of sayings go, "those who want everything die of anger", and "those who want everything, lose everything". Let others earn money too, and study your fanbase to constantly offer the entertainment your followers like: "the drop digs the stone by falling not twice, but often". Don't try and follow every trend, since many have failed by taking too many different paths. No one, however, has ever failed by doing too little.

I will now talk about give an influencer I know who posts video tutorials on mechanical watches: he's an expert at that, he knows that market very well and keeps up with current trends. He also benefits a lot from that, both in terms of income and online reputation. However, he once watched some popular videos about jewelry and he thought it was a much higher-paying niche than he one he was working in. He therefore decided to jump on that trend, even though he knew nothing about it: his contents were suddenly poor and didn't attract many new viewers. Some of his fans even unsubscribed from his channel as they found his new contents uninteresting. All of this to say, Finally, do not be fooled by envy and your desire for success; don't chase new trends just because they seem successful. Concentrate on one or two niches based on your own knowledge, try and offer quality entertainment every day for your fanbase. It will surely pay you back much more than constantly changing your content. Generally, anyone who wants to get rich in no time, fails; if you want to get rich, work hard and be content with modest but constant earnings. In the long run, they will be more rewarding than a single video with 10 million views. Schopenhauer said, "Wealth is like sea water: the more you drink, the more you get thirsty, and the same goes for fame".

5 STRIVE FOR CONSTANT IMPROVEMENT

The influencer must preserve his reputation; this way, followers can become more and more loyal and over time even hero-worship him.

When reviewing an electronic product, try to be as objective as possible, otherwise you'll lose the trust of your fanbase, which is essential in this job. This will also benefit you in the long run, because if you build your reputation day after day in an ethical way you will get more sponsorships by quality brands. I therefore suggest that you avoid sponsoring products of dubious origin or quality. This is even more true for those who advertise beauty products such as creams, perfumes, shampoos, conditioners, and so on.

Another real-life example will help. A client of mine used her channel to advertise a shampoo from a new brand which was still unknown in Italy. She took a commission based on how many articles he sold through an affiliate link. A customer whose hair had been damaged by the product sued him and he had to pay a lot of money because of that. It also cost her her online reputation. Now she is rebuilding her brand in a new niche, trying to correct that mishap. Therefore, you should always pay attention to the products you choose to advertise and try to be honest with your followers.

Remember to strive for constant improvement. The lights, the audio, the editing, the contents, the topics, the timing are all things that you must try to improve over time. Always the performance of each and every video, and study whether changes bring about more interactions. The faster you manage to reach your fans, the more the market is hungry for our content. That means you're doing a good job.

Be meticulous, take care of every single detail and aim for perfection in what you offer. Details make the difference between a sloppy, low-quality product and an excellent one. Be methodical in keeping track of any changes you make: if you change the microphone, keep track of whether your followers notice it and mention it in the comments. Positive reactions define new standards and encourage you to look for the next element to improve. Remember that big changes always happen one step at a time, or, as my mentor always says, "Even climbing the highest mountains takes one step at a time".

6 MONITOR YOUR ONLINE PERFORMANCE

There is a wonderful and easily accessible tool that allows you to keep track of your activities and earnings, of your online performance. You can organize and analyze large amounts of data, perform simple and complex calculations, keep track of all kinds of information and draw interactive graphs in a simple and professional way. This tool is better known as "electronic spreadsheet" and is available in many different free versions.

Knowledge of its basic functions is a must-have skill for any modern entrepreneur. In case you lack it, I suggest you attend some courses. The organization of your working week will benefit a lot from using electronic spreadsheets, and you will also be able to monitor your improvements over time. I don't know any successful entrepreneur, regardless of his field of expertise, who doesn't use them on a daily basis.

Let's see together how you can structure your control panel. There must be a first sheet, called DASHBOARD, which will indicate your status according to your goals, i.e. your BUDGET. The second and third spreadsheets will be called INCOME and OUTPUT. There, you will create some tables whose columns represent the weeks in a year and whose rows stand for incomes and expenses. These lines must be worked on in pairs, with a forecast line and a real one for each item. First of all, take the time to fill in the INCOME and OUTPUT sheets with forecast data or do the budgeting activity. The boxes for the real data will be left blank and filled in throughout the year as you collect the data. You should be as realistic as possible; when in doubt, underestimate your income and overestimate your expenses. This is a very complex business, and even the best managers in the world often get their forecasts spectacularly wrong. Based on my personal experience, I recommend doing this task every two weeks. For each box you fill out, note and explain why you think that value is correct. In the following days, double-check them and find out whether your evaluation was realistic or not. This multi-step procedure will allow you to be more objective in your evaluations and less dependent on your mood.

In the INCOME and OUTPUT sheets, at the end of the columns indicating the weeks, create a total column and do the same for the rows, taking care to report a forecast total and a real one. On the dashboard page, you will only report the total summary data, both forecast and real. You will therefore be able to monitor you actual performance with the help of some simple graphs. This exercise is quite motivational, since it helps personal growth.

As the weeks go by, keep both tables, INCOME and OUTPUT, updated, adding the actual values recorded. If you find yourself with unforeseen expenses, add 0 to the forecast box and fill the box dedicated to the real data. If this is your only source of income, you should put down the expenses for food and lodging in the OUTPUT spreadsheet, even if you live with other people. This will help you define the limits of your financial independence and the actual profitability of your business.

An essential rule of budgeting is to never change the forecasts once the budget is finished. You will often be tempted to adjust your previous forecasts to bring them closer to reality. Some people convince themselves that there are some particular cases where the budget needs to be revised. So I invite you to not give in to the temptation to change your budget, since the aim of this tool is to help and encourage you to persevere, to keep being productive and, therefore, to make your profession profitable.

I also suggest you to set an income corresponding to at least 1.2 times the expenses when you use the BUDGET tool for the first time. Thus, if you manage to stay within the budget, you'll have a margin of 20%; otherwise, you'll need this margin to avoid any loss.

What can you do in the event of a large deviation from the forecast budget? In the event that your expenses are much higher than what you had thought, you must evaluate whether they resulted in relatively higher incomes or not. If they generated more income and you still have a positive profit, you don't have to worry. If the outgoings went up and your income is less than or equal to the budget, you must decrease or postpone your expenses for a while until you're back on track.

If your income is much lower than expected, you'll need to find a way to increase it. You can open new channels or increase the quantity of content you offer, or even improve its quality. It should be said that it pays more to improve the quality of your product or service than to increase its quantity, even if it is a longer process.

Once you're familiar with electronic spreadsheets, you can improve and change them according to your needs. You can purchase the basic document I created for you to use as a first approach to this tool for economic planning on www.meetyourhero.it.

7 THINK ABOUT THE FUTURE

Working as an influencer can make you earn a lot in a fairly short period of time. This is why it is important to think about your long-term economic goals as soon as possible. The same happens to the most famous sportsmen, whose careers are full of multimillion-dollar contracts. However, even they can suffer abrupt setbacks due to sudden injuries, which can radically change their income stream. Moreover, their average career span is twelve years, and their earnings aren't always the same. Financial planning is therefore the first step to take when identifying what your savings and investment goals are. It requires an analysis of your financial situation, and, most of all, of the flow of income and expenses and your consequent saving capacity. This is the best way to monitor your spending habits in order to organize them in the most efficient way. Furthermore, it is important to correct any waste of resources in favor of more important and rewarding goals. As Warren Buffett said, "A good entrepreneur spends only what is left after saving". So here's a brief guide for identifying your goals, and therefore what your financial savings should be.
We all have life goals that can be achieved through financial resources to achieve. They can be either small and short-term, like going on holiday, or greater and long-term, like buying a house or getting a degree.
Different saving methods are therefore required for every need, both in terms of the amount to save and the financial instruments that should be available.

It is advisable to save a smaller amount of cash for contingencies and some short-term expenses.

Other objectives require tools offering returns through investments as to not have to rely on the money that has already been saved over time.

Write a list of goals that you set out to achieve, but remember it is a work in progress and can be changed and updated. Set a deadline by which you would expect to reach each goal and organize the list by putting the short-term ones first. The basic rule to follow is to save money starting from the bottom of the list: you must always make sure that long-term goals are funded by your savings.

In case you don't have enough resources to set aside for all your goals, you should postpone the short-term ones for a few months or even lower your standards.

For instance, if your short-term goals include a one-month trip to Australia and a retirement fund is your long-term goals, and your financial resources aren't enough for both, you will have to postpone or shorten your holiday.

Remember to proceed step by step and don't set impossible goals if your income is still low. You will always be able to update and improve your list as your financial resources grow by adding, improving or anticipating the goals you set for yourself.

The best balance should be the following: 40% for bills, costs, food and lodging; 15% for leisure (these expenses can be expendable in favor of long-term goals); 10% for a supplementary retirement fund; 10% fund for 7-year goals; 5% for a liquidity fund, 5% for an investment fund, 5% for a contingency fund and 5% for insurance. This breakdown of every possible expense works best for monthly incomes of less than 6000 €.

Larger monthly incomes (> 10,000 €) will lead to a different budget breakdown: 20% for bills, food and lodging; 10% for leisure, 15% for a supplementary retirement fund; 20% fund for 7-year goals; 10% cash fund, 10% for a contingency fund and 15% for insurance and investments.

These breakdowns are valid if you live in a European country. If you don't, they must take into account local financial law: for instance, at least 30% of one's budget is usually spent on health insurance in Canada and the USA.

As far as currencies are concerned, it is better to deal with stable (that is, not undergoing significant fluctuations) and recognized ones such as the US dollar and the euro. Local currencies from warring countries or nations with unstable governments should be avoided instead.

You should not hold cash, as to reduce the risk of scams or thefts. It is safer to trust a bank with your money. Avoid payments in cryptocurrencies since they're still unstable and could turn out to be damaging to one's personal finances. If you want to deal in cryptocurrencies, do it with awareness and invest only a small part of your savings. As far as your income is concerned, make sure you're paid with a stable and concrete currency that can be spent anywhere in the world.

A word to those who are starting their influencer business. Remember that this is a real job, so as soon as you have the chance, open a VAT number and keep up with your taxes. The sooner you'll do it, the easier it will be for you to understand that it is your creativity that makes you earn an income. It will also push you to create better content and improve your online performance.

8 LOOK FOR VALID COLLABORATORS

Whether you are a professional influencer with millions of followers on Instagram, TikTok and YouTube or a struggling rookie, you will have to get help from someone in the many daily tasks to be performed. If you have managed everything, from content creation to video editing, from sponsor search to marketing campaign design, up to now, you should consider looking for collaborators to help you share that burden. This does not mean that should delegate everything, but only some tasks.

A client of mine with an Instagram profile about exotic travels and 55,000 followers was able to post one video per week. He had excellent sponsors and his earnings were high, but he asked me how to improve his online performance and reduce worktime. We found out that he spent most of his time editing his video with limited skills and tools. I therefore suggested that he find a freelancer who would only work on editing the contents he produced. We found three different freelancers and tested them on the same job. The one most in tune with my client was hired for a long-term collaboration. Almost a year in, my client manages to produce between 6 and 8 video contents per month by working for only six hours a day. His lifestyle has improved and his channels gained 35% more viewers. That's what I call a double win.

You should try and follow his example. Identify the skills you lack and look for one or more collaborators with whom you can share the work. You'll be able to manage your days in a less stressful way and focus on what you do best.

You can find collaborators online on sites like www.freelancer.com, www.addlance.com, www.freelanceboard.it, www.upwork.com. No matter the figure you're looking for, test several candidate on the same project and then find the one who fit your needs the best. Once you've done that, contact him to offer a long-term collaboration. Creating a lasting working relationship will guarantee many things (faster response times, lower costs and consistency in what is offered) and also save a lot of time, since your collaborator will get to know your needs and your workstyle and provide a service that meets your expectations.

Remember that building a long-term relationship is not a quick process, but it can take up to six months or more of working together to start paying off. My personal experiences have led me to realize that there are two types of collaborators.

The creator is the most capable figure you can find, but he is difficult to manage; he is an independent figure, capable of creating projects, focused on the goal. He's usually self-taught, and if you don't engage him properly you will lose him.

Performers are easier to find than creators, but they must be trained, motivated and somehow controlled. I advise against hiring this type of collaborators directly: it is a feature of human nature to settle down and stop being very productive as soon as we realize that, whatever happens, we will get paid.

Keep your collaborations on a supplier customer plan: if your partner is no longer up to the task, you can easily switch suppliers. For the same reason, if you have an adequate amount of work, I advise you to assign more than one collaborator to each task. Thus, if a collaborator is unable to help you, you can have another take care of that job. Therefore, according to your needs, you will create a network of trusted collaborators, but you should never depend entirely on one of them. As Seneca said, be careful not to be hard-hearted when paying them. Pay them the right amount of money and don't overspend.

9 RESPECT THE COMMITMENTS YOU MADE

A good entrepreneur knows and manages his funds and pays debts quickly. All my mentors keep up to date with their business accounts on a daily basis. They taught me that it is important to be constantly aware of your income and expenses. You too should treasure their teaching and make sure that you keep your promises, as to not to damage your reputation. You should look for the same behavior when scouting for new clients and sponsors. In the world of influencer marketing, contact between suppliers and customers is distant or even absent more often than not.

Remember who pays your salary: the sponsor (that is, a company advertising a product) hires you to influence your fanbase and persuade them to buy something. You should therefore be honest with your followers, since their loyalty allows you to have access to sponsors, and refuse any collaboration that goes against your ethics.

If you can, choose what message you will convey to your fans and don't spoiler their user experience. Just as you are respectful of the commitments you make to your sponsors, you should also expect your customers to respect you.

When you can't get paid upfront, set a date by which the payment must be made and make sure that such a delay does not last more than 30 working days from the issuance of the invoice. In fact, I learned from experience that the longer the payment delayed, the more the customer considers himself entitled to request payment.

You can deal with such clients by insisting on calling and emailing them so they can pay you as soon as possible. Don't carry out other tasks while you're still unpaid, as scammers often force you to do that and bind you to them forever. It is very difficult to escape such a trap without losing money.

If more than 30 working days have passed since the deadline and this has not yet been done, I advise you to pursue legal action and contact a lawyer who will know what to do and relieve you from the stress of having to face this difficult situation.

Finally, I advise you to protect yourself from any scam by making every new customer pay you in advance.

10 THE QUALITIES OF THE GOOD INFLUENCER

Influencer marketing has recently become increasingly widespread. In fact, companies find it very important to identify the right influencer for their niche and target audience.
What are the qualities of the ideal influencer? How does an influencer stand out from his competitors and show he's able to influence his fanbase?
As their name suggests, they're great communicators who can affect their followers' choices and lifestyles. Starting out in this field of work, however, isn't easy: it requires having an interesting personality, charisma and authority, as well as specific social and professional skills.
Therefore, this work consists in being able to influence people's decisions based on their passions and interests. Usually, to be successful, you'll need to be able to find your own voice and create a true relationship with your followers. That way, your influence will be effective.
The most suitable qualities to the world of influencer marketing are constancy and moral integrity.

Serenity of the soul is very rare, especially nowadays. It should be a quality of every living being, but it takes people active and constant effort to achieve it. Serenity is not acquired overnight or by doing an exercise, but it is an inner reality that grows every day thanks to the choices one makes. Serenity means a greater awareness and knowledge of oneself and of the world around us. Being aware of living in peace helps us find the key to understanding what is happening around us, the best and most objective way to analyze and face what happens. Overcoming problems in the calmest and most optimistic way possible allows you to achieve serenity even in the face of injustice. The conscience of a pure soul provides complete serenity to those who follow an ethical/moral code and strive for intellectual honesty. Accepting everyday reality leads to serenity. Living well with yourself, with others and with nature leads to the truth and therefore to serenity.

This term describes an emotional condition that results in a state of calmness that is so deep that it is not subject to mood swings (both positive and negative) that could disrupt it. As Cicero said, "It is proper to a strong and constant soul to not be upset in adversity and to not rise in prosperity". Serenity is essential for one's emotional well-being; according to some studies, it is fundamental element of happiness. I suggest you exercise every day to pursue an inner serenity, this can be done with specific exercises or through a healthy and non-competitive athletic practice in the open air.

Constancy and discipline are two intertwined virtues that lighten and improve our lives and allow us to get out of serious individual and collective problems. Blessed are those who know how to use and combine them and manage to never waste them. As Plutarch said, "Strength is more powerful and more effective than any violence". Perseverance and discipline help you to succeed at work and in romantic relationships and face any kind of emergency. Perseverance must be the basis of your working method: without it, you risk losing everything, including your best qualities and talents. Constancy is self-discipline, and therefore awareness and a sense of proportion. Here, what counts is the rhythm, the dedication with which you carry out your project, rather than the end result. You must be ready to face huge obstacles, to find energy where strength tends to decrease, to recover, to start again when you fall. Constancy is the drop that hollows out the stone not by hitting once or twice, but multiple times on the same spot. Working as an influencer requires tenacity is needed, especially when results don't come easily. You need energy and you shouldn't waste it: the more gradual professional growth is, the more solid and lasting it will be. Shortcuts never get you far, and they often lead you to the wrong path. Talent, creativity, natural predisposition are all winning factors, but in the end it is constancy that makes the difference.

Reading biographies about past and present athletes, I found out that they all share a schedule of consistent training, regardless of injuries or periods of time off. For instance, Cristiano Ronaldo, one of the best football players at the moment, is still a fearsome player despite being older than the average athlete. Dedication, discipline and healthy habits are the secrets of his success. So I suggest you to act not in haste, but with constancy.

Moral integrity is one of the most important qualities that an entrepreneur and a leader should have, so it is essential to understand why. In this era of instant gratification, of the 'here and now', of easy solutions, finding people who are completely faithful to healthy and self-determined principles, is not a trivial matter. Having moral integrity means being dutiful, following the rules and respecting authorities. It also means doing the right thing when no one is watching, when there is no camera recording it. Feel in your heart that you are proud of yourself for how you're making a living. Since you have to establish a bond with your fanbase, it is necessary that you are honest in your actions and in your life choices. Kindness is a synonym of moral integrity. If you always behave kindly, you'll never have to regret it. You will even benefit from it. Being kind improves your mood you're your relationships. If anyone takes advantage of your moral integrity or your kindness, keep in mind that he will harm himself more than you. Stay true to your principles, so that no one can criticize you. When you doubt the morality of your actions of behaviors, it usually means that they're not moral.

Keep in mind that you have two options: you're either proud of something and talk positively about it with your family and closest friends, or you're ashamed of it and are uneasy talking about it. Remember this when making a decision, and make sure you're setting a good example for your followers.

11 CULTURES

Culture is the set of knowledge, norms, values, traditions and skills that define a society or a group of people. It also includes the arts, literature, music, history, philosophy and sciences. Cultured people have an advantage in the business world because of their deeper and more complex understanding of the social, cultural and political issues that affect business activities. Moreover, they tend to be more flexible and able to adapt to complex situations, using their knowledge to make informed decisions and solve problems creatively. Furthermore, culture can help build stronger interpersonal relationships and communicate effectively with people from different cultures.

Culture is everything for an entrepreneur, but above all for a human being. It can be hoarded, but it can't stolen.

The word "culture" comes from "cultivate", referring to the knowledge of a historical legacy which is made up of the knowledge, opinions, beliefs, customs and behaviors of a population. Culture is your property and you can improve it, day after day, at any age. So, if you want to become a good influencer, you should not only be a charismatic leader and an imaginative person and manage yourself, but also – and above all – someone wanting to know other cultures. Knowledge of the English language, which is now essential for communicating online all over the world, is therefore essential. It will allow you to stay up to date with new customs and trends of any kind. English is now the quintessential global language. In addition to being not that hard to learn, it is the primary language in business, education and the media. This means that learning English can make it easier for people to experience another culture directly.

Once you have a good grasp of the English language, you will be able to access a wide range of sources od information such as books, articles, films, songs and television programs in English. This will allow you to learn more about the culture, history and customs of English-speaking countries. This language is also often used as the common language for international relations, which means that people who speak English have a better chance of communicating and working with people from other cultures.

Furthermore, English is a very important language for most professions, especially those dealing with global economy and international communications, as it allows access to a wide range of working, business, and educational opportunities.

Culture can benefit successful entrepreneurs in several ways. For instance, it can provide a deeper understanding and awareness of the market and the people operating in it. It also increases creativity and the ability to think outside the box when tackling problems of any nature. Improving your communication and leadership skills can help create an inspiring work environment and can also allow you to build long-lasting and positive relationships with business partners and stakeholders by providing a positive image for their companies and attracting the best talents and clients.

12 LEARN HOW TO STREAM

To do a live stream, you'll need many things, such as:
- A webcam or video camera to capture the video.
- A computer or mobile device to stream the video.
- A stable, high-speed Internet connection.
- A streaming software to broadcast the video over the Internet.

The skills you need to run a good stream are even more important. As Dame Margaret Drabble said, "Public speaking is the art of finding out what to say at the right time". Here are the most important skills to have when making excellent live streams.

Organize your work environment well: make sure you have everything you need for the broadcast, such as good lighting and quality audio. Use a capture card, as it will allow you to capture video and audio directly from external sources such as your game console or mobile device.

Use a quality microphone: it will help you deliver clear, clean audio to your viewers.

Keep up the pace, try and be composed and measured in your words. Avoid playing games or moving your hands and feet too much: that's a sign of nervousness and can lead people to make fun of your reputation.

Be engaging: interact with your viewers during the live stream, invite them to ask questions and answer as soon as possible. Use these strategies to interact with viewers during a live stream.

1 - Interact with them through comments: during the live stream, answer questions and comments from viewers in

real time. This will show them that you are attentive and interested in them, and will encourage their participation.

2 - Ask questions and ask for opinions: asking viewers to share their opinions or thoughts on the topic covered during the live broadcast allows you to pause for a moment while talking and to understand your followers' point of views on that topic.

3 - Create a sense of community: use chat tools to create a sense of community among your viewers and encourage conversation between them, but keep the tone in check because of potential haters and ban them if necessary.

4 - Use interactive elements: polls, quizzes and multiple-choice questions encourage viewers to participate and make the live broadcast stand out by being more engaging.

5 - Answer the viewers' questions sincerely: during the broadcast, answering the viewers' questions gives them a sense of participation and involvement. Unlike those answers given in a later video, more immediate responses are better for your online reputation.

6 - Call to action: ask your viewers to share the link to the live stream with their friends to convince them to subscribe your channel or purchase a product related to the broadcast.

7 - Use visual and audio effects: it can make live broadcasts more engaging and attract more viewers.

8 - Involve guests, speakers or commentators: it allows you to make your live broadcast more interesting, to diversify the content offer and to attract new followers from your guest's channel.

9 - Use overlays: add overlays like text and images to your stream to make your content more interesting. Video transitions can also create a very professional effect.

Finally, organize your working day; use a broadcast timetable to plan your content and make sure you cover the main important topic you want to discuss. Be professional: respect your viewers and maintain a serious demeanor during the broadcast. Live streams are important tools for any influencer, so try and schedule at least one a week as to maintain personal contact with your followers.

13 WHAT MAKES A COMPANY MARKETABLE

Goodwill is the amount of money a buyer is willing to pay for the rights to use and continue another person's existing business. In other words, it represents the value of the brand, its customer relationships and the reputation of the entire business. Goodwill may be included in the selling price when a business is transferred to a buyer. This can be an important evaluation factor when buying or selling a business, as it represents its ability to generate future income. Selling your influencer business can be a complex process and require time and effort. Here are some steps you can take to do that.

Evaluate your business and determine its value by taking into account your followers, your social media presence and your reputation in the industry. There are some special agencies that can help you doing that. Identify the type of business or buyer who may be interested in acquiring your business. Create a sales package that includes detailed information about your business, your followers, and your social media presence. Promote it on your channels and platforms to grab the attention of potential buyers and to let your fanbase know your intentions. You will need to negotiate with potential buyers to determine the price and terms of the sale. Finally, you will be able to seal the sale in a safe and legal way, using a sales and purchase contract and involving a lawyer or financial advisor. It's important that you follow these steps carefully to make sure that your influencer business is sold efficiently and that you get paid what you deserve.

A suitable alternative to selling is bequeathing your influencer business. Your natural heir could be a child or grandchild who has a similar ability to connect with followers as you do. Zig Ziglar said, "The real legacy you can leave your children is not only your money, but also your values, your principles and your work ethic." Bequeathing an influencer's social channels can be complex and require proper planning. First, you need to create a will where you should specify who you want to inherit your social channels and how you want them to be managed in the future. You must also appoint someone you trust person as the heir to your social channels, since they will be responsible for their management.

You should provide the heir with the information needed to access your accounts and authorize them to manage them in the future.

You need to prepare a strategy to allow the heir to continue your influencer business and keep your followers loyal to your channel.

Warn your followers and inform them of the steps you are taking to ensure the continuation of your influencer business. Introduce your heir gradually in order to study your subscribers' reaction and take corrective measures if necessary. It is also important that you arrange a meeting with a lawyer or financial advisor to make sure that your wishes are respected and that your social media channels will be managed appropriately in the future. Keep in mind that some countries may have restrictive laws regarding inheritance.

Unfortunately, the influencer business generates a low-value goodwill, so I advise you to pay particular attention to the fifteenth chapter of this essay, which is dedicated to financial planning.

14 PRIVATE LIFE

Private life outside social networks is essential for people's emotional and mental health. Thanks to the constant and more frequent use of social networks, there is often a tendency to replace real relationships with virtual ones, which is something that can have negative effects on one's psychological health and quality of life. Love, affection and mutual support are essential for our personal growth and development, since they provide a sense of security and belonging and help build healthy and lasting relationships. Private life outside social networks offers the possibility of building these genuine relationships based on communication and sharing meaningful moments. It is important that you give time and attention to them, whether they involve friends, family or partners. The same goes for the need to disconnect from digital devices and spend time doing self-care and building better social relationships. Therefore, private life outside social networks and affections plays a fundamental role in our lives, providing emotional stability, support and meaning. Giving time and attention to these relationships can improve your mental health and quality of life. The role of family in Generation Z (people born between 1997 and 2012) is still very important, even if it may differ from that of previous generations like mine. First, family is a source of emotional support and comfort for its members, as it provides them with a support network and a safe environment. Furthermore, it gives them values that will guide them in life and show them how to behave in society. If you aspire to become an influencer and be independent from your family, you may be wondering whether it's better to form your own family or to live alone. Nowadays, many people like being in complete control of their lives and don't want their freedom to be limited by a romantic relationship. Others, on the other hand, are busy pursuing personal goals like careers or traveling and don't have the time nor the energy to be in a relationship. Finally, others simply prefer being alone and do not want to share their living space with anyone else.

A social nature is a distinctive trait of the human being that has allowed them and society to evolve. People need to interact with others to satisfy their social, emotional and cognitive needs, and they need to belong to a group to feel safe and secure. Social interaction is important for the development of interpersonal relationships and for creating one's individual identity. Furthermore, it has proved to be essential for the survival and development of the human species, since in the past it led to the sharing of resources, skills and knowledge to solve problems. For these reasons, even if you want to remain single or live a free love life, you should still consider sharing your house with a roommate. Dividing expenses like rent, utility bills, and food expenses can help you save money and manage your finances in a more efficient way. You will also have someone to talk to and with whom you can share your worries. Household responsibilities can be divided equally between roommates, making everyone's lives easier and less stressful. I advise against sharing your house with too many people, since it is more harmful than beneficial.

If you want to start a family of your own, take these reflections into consideration. Choosing who to start a family with is an important and personal decision that requires time, thought and consideration. Choose someone with whom you have many things in common and with whom you can share your interests, values and goals, with whom you can communicate well and who is able to listen and respect your thoughts and opinions. Look for someone who supports and encourages you during hard times and who helps you achieve your goals; someone who is reliable and committed and who is always there for you. Choose someone who has similar expectations to yours about marriage and family life.

It's important that you and your partner share common values and communicate well and that there is a balance between giving and receiving. There is no magic formula for choosing the right person, but you can make an informed and satisfying choice by taking the time to get to know yourself and your potential companion.

Privacy is a fundamental right for every person, and this also applies to influencers. Public figures are under constant scrutiny from the media and the public, and this can make it difficult for them to preserve their partners' privacy. It is important for their emotional and mental health: constant exposure to the public and the media can cause stress and anxiety and undermine their partner's quality of life. Protecting your partner's privacy ensures that your relationship remains private and unaffected by outside pressure. Romantic relationships must be based on trust and communication, and these factors can be compromised if they're exposed to the public.

Furthermore, maintaining your partner's privacy also protects their reputation and business. Their private lives can be distorted or misrepresented in the media, which can negatively affect their work and career. Finally, protecting your partner's privacy shows that you respect them and your relationship with them.

All things considered, protecting your partner's privacy is essential for their emotional and mental health, as it makes sure that your relationship remains private and healthy, that partner's reputation and business are safe and that you are respectful and considerate towards them.

15 INVEST WISELY

Influencers and entrepreneurs should accumulate the capital they manage to earn and make sure that it can yield additional capital in the future. Online success can be short-lived, and users are always looking for new and better things thanks to the increase in competition. This makes it difficult to maintain a dominant position on the online scene for long. Social networks have become an important part of people's online lives, but their popularity of a particular social network can quickly fade thanks to different new trends. Similarly, websites that were once the first in their field may now be replaced by new ones with better functions or a more attractive design. The fickle nature of users plays another important role in this. For instance, viral videos can become popular in no time, but their popularity can fade just as quickly. This is why you must be able to accumulate and invest the capital you can earn, especially in moments of euphoria. Remember not to go on spending sprees and wasting money on cars or luxury homes just because you've had 3 or 4 consecutive months of excellent earnings. Many influencers or VIPs have lost their fortune in reckless spending.

The stock market is one of the most popular investment options for investors looking for opportunities to grow their capital. Shares represent an ownership stake in a company and can be bought and sold on a regulated market. Capital growth opportunities in the equity market can be attributed to several factors. Publicly traded companies tend to grow and generate profits over time, which can lead to an increase in the value of the shares and therefore an increase in capital employed.

Dividends are another form of capital growth. Companies can distribute part of their profits in the form of dividends to shareholders, which means investors can receive regular cash flow from these investments.

The stock market is also affected by multiple factors such as economic growth, government policies, and global market conditions. They may affect the performance of the shares and therefore the growth of your invested capital. However, it must be kept in mind that the stock market also carries risks. The value of shares can be affected by factors such as an economic downturns, smaller corporate profits or unstable political conditions. Therefore, while the stock market offers many opportunities for capital growth, it is important for investors to understand the risks associated with this type of investment and to diversify their portfolio in order to avoid these risks.

I advise you to ask a financial advisor to follow you and adopt an accumulation plan which will help you invest your capital little by little and in a safe way. At the same time you will set aside part of your capital for any periods of economic hardship or for a project you're particularly interested in. Some of my clients have felt the need to take a gap year to get away from their stressful jobs and daily routine. Being constantly under the eyes of your followers can lead to serious psychological problems, since the pressure to maintain a positive public image on social media can cause stress and anxiety. Furthermore, the constant comparison with the seemingly perfect life of others can lead to develop some feelings of insecurity and dissatisfaction. Saving money for a gap year is an ambitious project that requires planning and financial discipline. It offers you the opportunity to travel, explore new cultures and recharge your batteries away from daily routine.

Another solution would be to stop working at all. The amount of capital needed to live happily without working depends on many factors such as the cost of living, lifestyle and personal needs. However, it is generally recommended that you have an amount of savings that covers at least 3-5 years of basic expenses, such as rent, utility bills, food and insurance. It's important to keep in mind that this is only a general guideline and that each person has unique financial needs and goals. Therefore, it is advisable to consult a financial advisor in order to establish a savings plan that is appropriate for your needs. In any case, it is important that everyone takes their financial circumstances into consideration and carefully plans their financial future to ensure a happy life without financial worries.

CONCLUSION

In conclusion, becoming an influencer can be an exciting and rewarding adventure, but it also requires a lot of effort and commitment. Remember that your true identity and worth do not depend on your popularity or your followers. Be yourself and embrace your unique strengths, as they are what make your content authentic and interesting to your fanbase. Constantly work on your personal growth and self-esteem, as this will help you better handle the pressure and challenges that can come with public life on social media.

Most importantly, don't forget to enjoy the ride and celebrate your success along the way. Remember that there is no magic formula for success, but your determination, creativity and ability to inspire others are the keys to becoming a successful influencer.

Always be proud of yourself and be true to yourself and the message you choose to convey to your followers, and the results will come.

Before ending this essay, I want to tell you how Australian ice skater Steven Bradbury won a gold medal at the Salt Lake City 2002 Winter Olympic Games. His story is an example of being stubborn when following one's dreams, despite the many obstacle life throws at people. Bradbury was an ice skater from a young age but faced many hardships throughout his whole career. He suffered from serious injuries and had to overcome personal and financial obstacles to continue pursuing his dream, but he never lost his passion and determination. His victory at the Salt Lake City Olympic Games was the highlight of his career and a testament to his determination to make his dream come true. Despite participating in a highly competitive contest and the odds being against him, Bradbury became the first Australian athlete to win a gold medal in the history of the Winter Olympic Games.

His story is an example of how determination and believing in one's dreams can help people overcome even the greatest challenges. It teaches us that no matter how difficult the circumstances, if we believe in ourselves and follow our hearts, we can achieve our dreams and be very successful. A little luck may help.

My dear reader, I wish you'll be successful in making your dreams come true.